The Dogs in My Life

The Supreme Master Ching Hai

Love Love

For Butterfly

and Peter, the stray well-mannered dog

For the dogs in my life

And all the animals alike

Despite the fact that we are an odd herd

with different species of dogs,

we all have one thing in common —

this beloved human "pet," we all own!

Inspired by the dogs

Compiled by

Supreme Master Ching Hai

And to all the dogs that I love:

1 Benny

2 Lucky

3 Happy

4 Hermit

5 Goody

6 Boyo

7 Lady

8 Pomas

9 Zolo

10 Hally

Home - Photos from:

Supreme Master Ching Hai

Crystal Vo

Victor Ngo

T. June

Thomas Lux

Steven Andre

Danny Vu

Words from a Child

These are the examples of what should be
The life of our friends, sweet animals.
Be it on land, on air or in the sea.
They should be loved, protected and cherished,
Just like the life that we so wish.

Dearest Heaven, Dear Lord of Karma
Please do love and care for all creatures
For it breaks my heart to see their plight.
I cannot bear to see them suffer.

There're plenty places in Heaven above
Take them all up, and give them love.
This's my little prayer for all beings:

Just your little Love and Compassion.
May all be well, live and let live.
All Love, all care and all forgive.

~ Supreme Master Ching Hai

The Story of the Human Saint We Adopted

Collectively written by Ten Lucky Canines

Benny, Lucky, Happy, Hermit, Goody, Boyo, Lady, Pomas, Zolo, and Hally

~ Compiled by Book Group

Our beloved human, or simply, our Mom, is also known by countless people in the world as Supreme Master Ching Hai. As a young child, She already showed signs that She was destined to become a Saint through Her natural great love for all beings, including us animals.

Since becoming an enlightened Master, She has devoted Herself to the teaching of the Quan Yin Method (an ancient meditation practice focusing on the inner Sound and Light) and the promotion of vegetarianism. She once said that if only one half of the world's people became vegetarians, we would have peace on Earth. The killing of animals for food has culminated in a violent atmosphere, which in turn sprouts violence, wars and misery among humans. Therefore, the lives of us animals and those of humanity cannot be separated.

To those who follow our human Saint, She might be a Master or a great teacher, but to us animals, She is just our loving Mom. She does all things a Mom does, like bathing us, cooking for us, singing to us, taking us for walks, and playing with us. We hope we can share Her love with all our animal friends in the world, and that the day will come when each and every one can live a life with an abundance of food, warm shelter, and love, the way we do.

With much love
To Humans and all.

Biography of The Supreme Master Ching Hai

The Supreme Master Ching Hai was born in Central Au Lac (Vietnam). At the age of eighteen, Master Ching Hai moved to England to study, and then later to France and then Germany, where She worked for the Red Cross and married a German physician. After two years of happy marriage, with Her husband's blessings, She left Her marriage in pursuit of enlightenment, thus fulfilling an ideal that had been with Her since Her childhood. This began a time of arduous pilgrimages to many different countries that ended only when She met a perfect living Master in the Himalayas. Master Ching Hai received the divine transmission of the inner Light and Sound, which She later called the Quan Yin Method. After a period of diligent practice, She attained Perfect Enlightenment.

To satisfy the longing of sincere Truth seekers, the Supreme Master Ching Hai offers the Quan Yin Method of meditation to people of all nationalities, religions and cultural backgrounds. Her message of love and peace brings spiritual liberation and hope to people throughout the world, reminding all to uphold Truth, Virtue, and Beauty in life.

1 BENNY   *01*

2 LUCKY   *95*

3 HAPPY   *181*

BENNY

Benny, my first "official" dog. Maltese.

Protective, loving, loyal and also sticky

(likes to stick close). He is a scholar, officially.

Nicknames: The Boss, The Alfa, Big Brother,

The Scholar.

He attended/graduated from a training school

named K-9 Cadet. The school was impressed

by his behavior and discipline. When he

graduated, I came to bring him home. The

teacher told him to lay down. He did. Anxious

to be in my arms, but "not allowed to walk"

by the teacher, he crawled toward me inch by

inch, like a trained soldier. And reached me in

the still "down" position, as the teacher and all

present shed tears of emotion. "My God! We

did not teach him this!"

Benny is very compassionate and caring. If someone is sad, he comes to offer comfort and love to that person till he or she is cheered up. One of my attendants used to play drama like crying, and Benny would always come to him and kiss him all over every time. Benny specially loves children and other animals. If he finds an injured bird or other, he will sit there on guard till I come over and take care of it. He is ever so quiet and gentle as not to frighten the wounded creature.

He loves Veggie Green Bones like crazy. But if I give with the intention to pacify him as I'm leaving the house (and him) to go out, he won't take the bone, but goes away from it into a corner and sulks! He sneaks to my place/bed anytime if let him, forsaking all comfort of his own bed/sofa.

Every time I came home, or let him in my room, he is excited like Heaven, rolling all over my bed, my sofa, or sleeping bag, or on the floor – just depends on what's available.

He is a loving being incarnate. He is a high-level soul who humbly plays the role of a little dog, just to love me.

In the beginning, there was solely me –
Benny the first and only.

Wait...for me!

I'm out here, Mom!

Who is the lucky guy?

My official photo at five months old.

Am I still visible in the white snow?
Luckily I have a red vest and black eyes,
black mouth and black nose.

(I also have black soles,
but they are not showing here though!)

This is Canada.
    I was five years old.
        Brrr···so cold!

Luckily we moved away in a few months though.

I was born in Florida.
Have never seen this white snow before!
The sun shines where me & Mom lived,
Even in the winter
except when we walked together
in the garden, or on the beach
I have always stayed indoors.

Just checking if snow is really as cold as people keep telling me.
One thing I tell you, it is very soft. I can dig easily.

Canada is really too "cool" !
Even for a "furry" like me!

We are happy happy!

Woa! Woa! Woa!

I own the whole green yard!

It's not my fault—
It's the mud
that I dug!

She still loves me though.

I don't like this "soap opera" stuff. Not a bit!

It ain't true. I'm not just a suit!

Does it have to be??

Well!...
OK.
I see the point.
It's a nice feeling
after bathing.

We are clean now!
(Well, till the next outing.)

Yeh! Get that sticky wreck
off my tender neck!

There!

  It feels

      better.

      Thanks

          Mother!

Why, but I don't worry about the future!
She is my future. 🩶

There, there···
A piece of sticky weed on my pretty hair again!
I told it that it is not welcomed!

I can't smile. My face is all dirt-smeared!

Well, okay! Here!
Happy?

stay in the present

Who am I?

Don't care!

Mom said to "stay in the present."

But I can't help thinking of the past!
That was a messy place
where I came from!
So confined!
So unkind!

See what I
    can dig up
        in the veg
            garden.

Ah!
Some potatoes!
Well,
I'll eat only
when it's cooked.

28

Sure are a lot
of plants
in here,
Mom!

A taste
of
natural
spring.
Refreshing!

Again potatoes!
And organic
    self(men)-farmed.

That was a lot of walking
and "working" I tell you!

Don't you envy me?
Actually, I'm helping Mom
with her office work!

We look like twins!
She is the neighbor girl! Pretty and frisky!

Yoo-hoo! I am here.

Yoo-hoo! I am here.

Yoo-hoo! I am here.

Is this camouflaging
or what?

I think it's more discreet here.

But it's safer here.

Now! Both smile for the camera!

"Sharing,"
caring...

Then came
another —
A poodle?!
No, a bijon!
"BEEJO...ONG"
OH LA LA!

Then another —
　　A mixed terrier!
　　　　Terrible!
　　　　　"Sharing, caring…"
　　　　　　I know all that!
　　　　　　　But…

Well!
I know
I am
petit.

But I'm
just 4
months
young.

It's not the food.
I wanna love.

I'll show you, newcomer.
Size doesn't matter.

You're strong,
but I'm smart.

This's meine!
Yours is bigger
over there!

We get on well though.

As long as
I am loved!

Ha ha!

I told you: I am the first!

No matter who comes into the herd!

Even in meditation.

This guy, Poodle or whatever,
is kinda weird, huh!

Why, you are "on" my bed!

(Well! Halfway through!)

Ain't it too "small" for you?

We get along pretty well.
Puh is kinda sticky though.
Must be our previous karma.

See what I mean by "sticky"?
Not only does he want Mom,
he also wants me!

We are always the best buddies!

Dear God!
When will it end—
the meditation?

　　　So we can go
　　　　running in the garden···

How about us two?

Sorry,
no more room for you,
Luck!

58

Leave me alone!
When I am chewing a "Greenie" veggie bone,
it's a "red" zone!

Wherever she is, it's Heaven inside out!

I am luving it. ♥

But...
Sometimes,
I feel
kinda...small

and unsure.

I am just wondering:
Who will free me
from the bonds of transmigration?

What's there
beyond the
darkness?

Are you sure no electricity?

What's out there, Puh?

Let's go find out!

Yeh, Mom unplugged it.

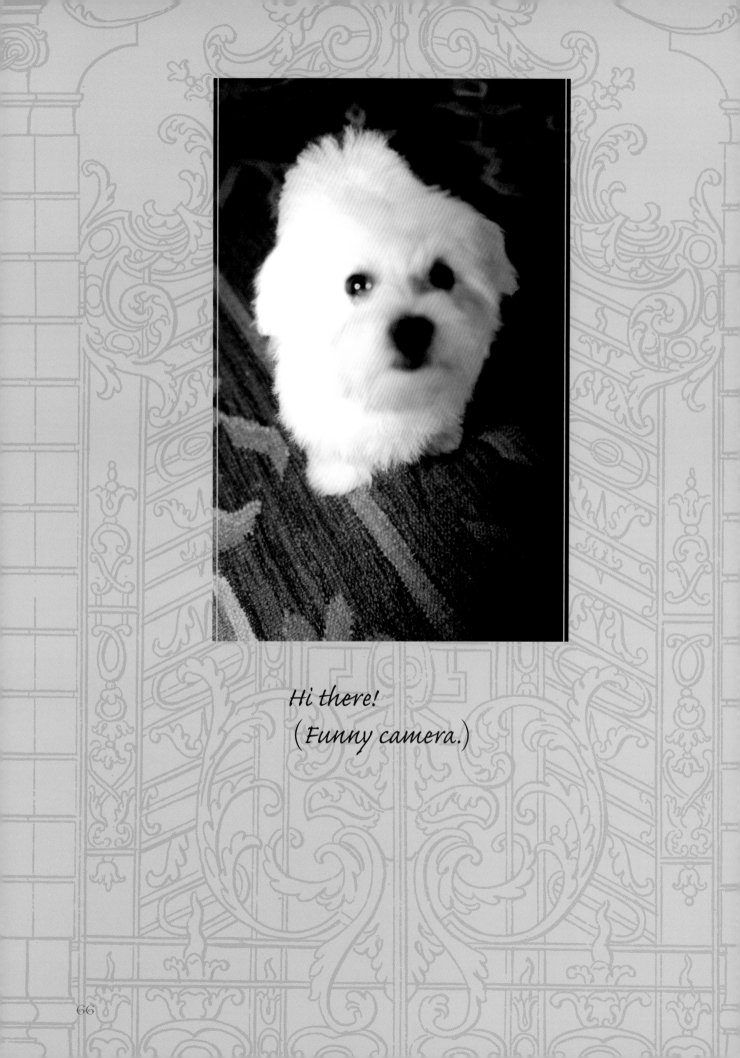

Hi there!
(Funny camera.)

And then
this one—
where does
the chap
come from?

Then again···this one! Oh dear Heaven!

Well, I can't complain!

Now, you see ?
Bigger and bigger family.
Crowded
but happy.

And they just laze around "my house."
I am tired
of telling them how.

Goody!
  Can you forget
      the shadows for once?

I wanna sleep.
Sleep is what we want!

Mom is out but she'll be back, Ben.
Don't worry!

The nearer, the better!

Wish they'd come down here to play with me for a while!

I don't look
like me···
Ah, this
haircut!
Mom said it'll
grow again.
(I hope!)

The future is
some interesting stuff
to think about, wuf?

What are you staring at?

Don't make me shy.

I'm in deep thinking

About the thing called life.

Yeh! This is life!
This is love!
This is truly Wof.

Ain't I cute?
Mom said so!

LAUGHTER IS

GOOD FOR HEALTH !

My Heaven!

My Heaven!

Even with the
whole flock
I feel all alone
without her.

Is Mom
coming
back
soon?

I'm used to the crowd
by now.
Yeh! And even this new wingy one!
        He's just so···sticky to Mom!

But I learnt to be sharing.
Mom said we have to love all beings.
So we are all vegetarian.

Ah-hah! Can't imagine!
The piglings have been here last night!
Even my territorial protection odor they'd defy!

Anyone home?

I'm done.
Let me in.

You see,

I am always "THE LOVED."

And I can prove it
right here!

(I don't get it
when other flocklings
proclaim the same thing!)

And I love TV.

He is only big,
But believe it
I control the whole situation!

He listens to me
all the time!

I also "fixed" this guy.
   We are "cool" really.
      He knows I'm the boss!

Zolo is his name. (Mom gave)

By the way,
he is the 9th in my flock.

There is one more!
I hope Mom stops!
I can't manage
A bigger herd!

This is Boyo, the⋯
let me see⋯ 7th or 8th or something like that!

What do you think we might find in those bushes, Bo?

LUCKY

Lucky was from a pound in Florida. He was on a "death row," very sick when he first came and had to receive emergency medical services as well as dental operations, for most of his teeth were decayed. He stunk like a dead corpse. He was afraid to be alone, but he is okay now.

He is loving, protective, and sticky.

Nicknames: Tongy, Oldman, Fruity (loves Fruits), Puh Puh, Pei Pei

Lucky was very sick when I got him from the pound, so we had to nurse him for 3 months.

During this time he was quaratined and I came daily to play with him in the pen, he loved to play with a tennis ball. Since that time, after he got well, he always sneaks into my bathroom, waits outside the shower till I open the shower door, then he throws the ball from his mouth into the shower, expecting me to play there!

Also, I gave him a special diet with lots of fresh fruits and vegetables, and since then he loves them so much that he won't eat without fruits and/or vegetables! He can "smell" fruits from miles, we joke!

We use fruit to tempt him to eat anything; even if he ignores his lunch, just wave a piece of apple in front of him, and then he'll eat the food, to take the "bribed" apple!

He can eat fruits any time of the day and night, and as big a quantity as a big human, if we let him! And he himself is my "Apple," beautiful with his big and innocent happy eyes, contrary to the sad look he had when we first met. We call him a "Ten Thousands Dollars Dog" because when I first got him he had to be rushed to all kinds of emergency clinics and dentists (the best and expensive of course).

It cost +$10,000 US to fix most of the problems that he had, in the beginning. Hence, the "Ten Thousands Dollars Dog." But to me, he is a treasure priceless beyond any price. And that's what I keep telling him, and he knows that too well. He is so affectionate – loves nothing better than sleeping on my lap, even forgoing meal time with fruits if I let him!

"You will
get well soon"

When I first arrived with all kinds of ailments
and red patches all over my body…

(I look like a hotdog, but not for eating!)

Mom dyed my hair all red with color of fruits to
cover the different discoloration parts on my hair.

I like it: I look better. I look cheerful!
                    And well kept! And special! ♥

It's squeezy,
but it's cozy.
I like it very!

It's okay.

I like the corner.

(I just feel like an omega.)

I'm OK, just like to "hang around."

When Mom got me from the pound,

and the death row, I was so…sick.

Mom and her aids nursed me for 3 months!

"You will
get well soon."

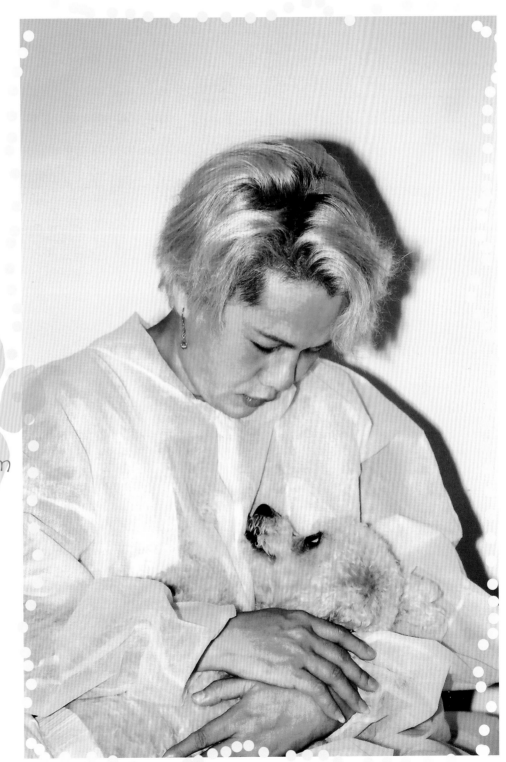

Yes, Ma'am

Don't you love all this!

Though I hadn't completely recovered.

I feel well!

I am

recovering…

Recovered! 🩷

It's me
The Lucky!

It's me alright!

Well and Alive!

Here, with Benny the buddy.

He looks happier normally.

in this world?

Anything last forever in this world, Ben?

Sadly, no! But yes, only in Heaven!

Whewph!...
Talk about playing!

And this is another buddy.

I became a veggie dog
- cool dog, not hot dog -
And I do meditate!
This photo proves it.

I am blissful

I am blissful.

I "don't sweat the
small stuff."
And I don't sweat the big stuff.
In fact I don't sweat at all.

Tête-à-tête

Three heads are better than one!

And we have a "cool" head atop.

One apple a day, keeps the vet away.

All is okay under the sun!

Guess

whose lap?

You are right!

Sorry! It's all
occupied!

"Me"? Can you find?

You are not taller than me.
Give up trying, Ben Honey!

Can you find me still?

But I keep thinking
after what happened,
will she really keep me?

Is it my second, third…
Or last sanctuary?

I mean, don't you…
kinda worry about
the future?
(once abandoned…)

"What's wrong, Luck?"

Nothing!
I'm haunted a
little by the past!

(This is how I looked even after one month of intensive care)

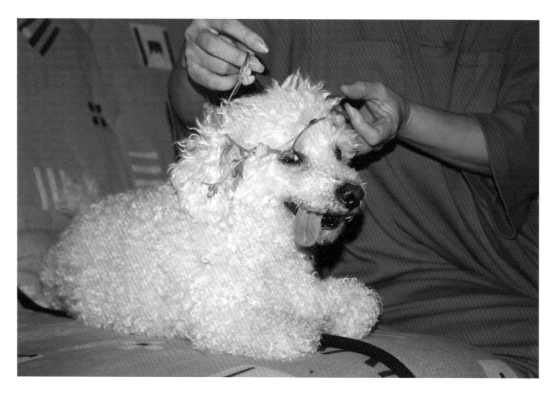

If you love me,

Make me pretty 💜

There! There!

I am pretty...

...much loved.

Man! Am I pretty!

And I am a star!

Yeh!
That's me,
alright!
I am
so…loved.

Ha! Ha! It's very funny!

157

Just think how I
looked before.

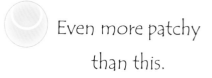 Even more patchy
than this.

And I was "gray"
when I first came!

Give me my favorite ball!

Now! Okay, please

You know what it feels like!

To have all that you desire.

I am loved! I know for sure.

(#1)

This photo I don't like.

This sure is better alright.
I don't like it when my head was cut off
in the picture #1 on the left side!

Life has been hard in my past.

But here is all soft now!

Yeh! It's me, Lucky.

Six months later.

(I know, I can't even recognize myself)

It's me again! The ever lucky-er.

(After having the best dentist, many vets and top groomer…)

The love that melts your heart!

And the love that melts your heart!

Even in my dreams I'm feeling the bliss.

Can't remember who this was in red!

I love Canada!

Oh! Canada! I love Canada!
Can you help put my tongue back in, yah?

We didn't stay long then.
Thanks Heaven!

What's wrong with my tongue?
I can re-tuck it no more!
It has never frozen before.

I don't want to remember
The freezing time ever.
But just to refresh your view,
I include here a few.

It's all worthwhile!

Wait for me!

I'm coming!

Oh… don't think
it's a good idea!

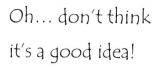

Almost there,
Mom!

I am not oldy.
It's the big lunch…
It's… it's the gravity!
It's the staircase!

A little help
won't hurt, Mate!

Well! It's all worthwhile!

To climb any mount!

We always feel
good good!

OK. OK.

Please, please,
can I have it now!!!

You know I love it.
Don't make me beg!

Ahhh......

Yem yem!
Chewing carrots will make you slim.

I think too much food
is no good for me.
Even though it is just Veggie!

I don't like this
at all
… not one bit.

Where is
my cushion??!
my blanket?

This is too "low-grass"
for a Princy like me!

Mom said:

"The meditator is happy

wherever he is!"

Yeh Yeh! But here I'd rather be.
Wouldn't ye?

(Can you spot 7 differences between the 2 photos?)
If yes! Reward yourself with a Poodle!

Buddies night or day,
Resting to while the time away.

Now this is more like it!

Don't you just "lap" this!

Absolutely in...

Zynzzz....

I could meditate standing!

And this is good for my soul!
Hug a dog and you'll know.

I think I am also a think-tank,
but I think I don't know what to think!

Yeah! Who doesn't have a bad hair day?
But we always feel good good!
Be it in summer breeze
Or in Winter Sun Rays.

A spiritual
practitioner
like…one
of my level (!)
Or higher

Feels comfy
anywhere!
Really.

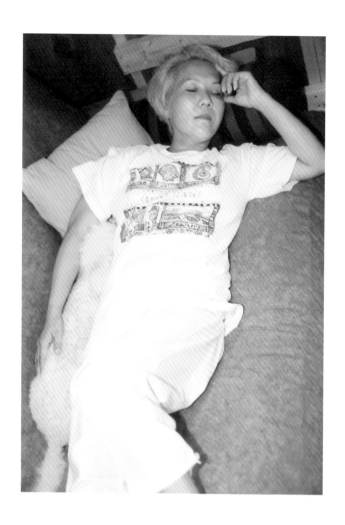

Nevertheless,
Her couch
is my couch.

Her house
is my house.

As long as I can lap around,

doesn't matter who is there!

I don't really care!

Watch me!

I won!

Never mind who says what.
I'm always at the top!

I like group photos!

Especially when I am all groomed
And with good people.

And a new buddy, guess who?
(A hint: he rattles)
I am hiding with him
under a cool table.

No no!

I look a little like him (Albert),

but we are not related!

Not the I.Q. part anyway.

Eh, maybe the tongue stuff

…and the head on a good hair day.

HAPPY

She was also adopted from a pound (same one as Lucky's). She was shy and reserved at first, but she's okay now. All the boys in the house love her. She talks with her expressive eyes. She loves all living & breathing humans, animals, also trees and the like. She's loving, loyal, protective, and sticky.

Nicknames: Princissa (Being Sissy), Gordita (Spanish for Chubby), Waggy (She wags the whole body not just tail), Caku (Before, loved to eat Gecko)

She has a way to greet me that no other dogs do. If she is in my bedroom alone at night, and I come in, she plays like an actor; she lowers her head, and lowers her behind, alternately jumping back and forth, right and left playfully, and throws her whole body at me sideways and keeps doing that till I ask her to stop and pet her; then she sits and kisses all over me and rolls over like other dogs. I can't really describe it well, 'cause she acts like a human knowingly and deliberately, and she "talks" with her body, with her expressive say-it-all eyes. She really does!

One time, I was somehow too burdened with pain. I let out some cry in my bedroom, and Happy was beside herself with panic! She ran around me and kept crying till I stopped. Lucky also threw himself on my lap and keep whining, too. Then both of them lay beside me for the whole night; they wouldn't leave. Other dogs also hung tight next to me!

Me too! You see...

I meditate "happy-ly."

and lappy-ly!

We do *"group meditation"* daily.

Life is...

a Song.

Or?
Is It?

What is life???

I hope life continues as it is.
Will it?
Is it my permanent home? Forever loved?

As it is right now,

life is going well.

I have buddies.

I have love…

Together, we feel… Wofe!

My new Mom loves me
for sure!

I am more sure
each day,
each minute,
each TREAT!

I am Happy.

Don't you recognize me?

I am still…Happy (not sad!)
I am just posing, acting pensive!

…Just a good actress!

Oh! Canada!

My paws never felt like this before!
What is this white stuff?
It came from nowhere!
Yesterday, it wasn't here!

Why does my butt feel cold, too!

I think if I stand too long like this,
   I will certainly become a statue!

Not a "Happy" one, though.

Where are you guys?
   It's not "cool" anymore!
      Would someone fetch my jacket?!

United we warm.

You that way, I this way.

Let's see if the snow
is whiter on the other side!

Why does

My butt!

Feel cold!

I'm just sitting the usual way!

Strange!

The longer I sit,
the colder it gets.

Changing position
doesn't help either!

I don't think it's a good idea to sleep here tonight.
Even if I dig a deeper hole,
or cover myself with a blanket of snow.

Home is always the best place!

Don't you agree?

"Do not disturb."

"It's written on the door!"

202

No room?

Ok! Ok! I'll stay down here.

Believe me, I am a lap dog. I'll fit in!

See?!

Told you, I am a lap dog.

"Of course, they are not real."

"We can't chase real animals here."
(I know!)

Say: "V E G G I E !"

Yum!

Can we share?
    Sharing is caring, Mom said!

I am an internationalist.
I am everywhere.
Especially at the location of treats.

Here, we can run forever.

I am the name (Happy)!

...But we can't run forever!

Whewph…need to nap.

Have I outgrown this sofa,
or has it become smaller?

I like to be "taken on a ride."
It's less tiring and energy-saving.
We all don't mind!

Too late!
They are always too fast.

Just to thank you, ma'am!

And I'll guard your dreams.

I know your love is equal for all of us.

But I worry.

Can I keep Mom forever?

Can I live forever with her?

What does the future life hold for me?
And my pack?

Will anyone ever live forever…?

I better just enjoy
the "now."
Mom said She will
definitely take me Home
to Heaven, where I belong!

Yoo Hoo! I spy.

Daily teeth brushed.
Nice smile.

And I am pretty.

I am photogenic

on both sides!

I love fresh air
and the sunshine.
It keeps my tan
beautifully alive!

In any posture,
I am always pretty and happy!

Ok,
I'll
smile.

Can't …   …keep …   …up any longer!

Goody buddy,
can you pay me some attention?

Or shadows are just your fix?
Say something nice at least!

I'll do
anything for
a veggie
green-bone!

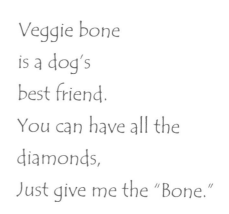

Veggie bone
is a dog's
best friend.
You can have all the
diamonds,
Just give me the "Bone."

Bedtime story
Is my fav. after Greenie.

...And what happened then
to Princess Snow White
After she met her charming Knight?

I know, they lived
happily ever after!
Or?

Join me, enjoy nature.

I'll just prove it, that...

...the grass is really greener on the other side.

The reposing
recluse.
The whole world
is mein.

The grass is nicer over there.
But I am cooler over here.

Me? No..o…
I am not fat!
It's just the blacky
He is too skinny!

You won, Ben!

Yeh! It feels good to win, I know.

Wow! Ben, it's a happy fairy "tail" that you told.

Where is
everyone?
Come back!
Don't leave me
All alone.

Can I kiss him?

Wof! He likes me!

Waky waky

Wr…Do I have to?
Time to lunch already?

Have I been dreaming all this?

EPILOGUE

The book can only describe a fraction of what an extraordinary being a dog can be - only dog keepers know about it.

Each dog merits a whole big book to detail all his life and characters. But, all in all, dogs are a very noble race of beings.

I hope to let the readers enjoy some glimpse of the beautiful ways that dogs walk the Earth with us, and through them, understand more about other beings.

I want you to know that, we (all souls) choose to incarnate in the physical realm through a variety of forms. But all beings are like us. They are born to live out their time, to contribute to a colorful life on this planet. It thus behooves us to be their good co-inhabitants, with all due respect, peace and love.

If, in our lifetime, we chance to have a personal relationship with anyone in the animal kingdom, consider ourselves blessed and lucky!

Master 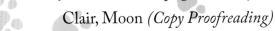 the following individual for their meticulous assistance:

Crystal Vo, Victor Ngo, T. June, Thomas Lux, Steven André, Danny Vu *(Cameramen)*

Annie Yu, Nadir Yen, Chien Wei Ba-Li, Kim Cheng, Jackie *(Design and Layout)*

Gary Lai, Nadir Yen, Yu Hui-Chun, Wang Bor Tang, Sofia, Jackie *(Graphic Design)*

Lynn McGee, Jane Chu, Wenqing Li, Becky Chen, Sun Wang, Clair, Moon *(Copy Proofreading)*

"…And for permeating your work with love"

~ Supreme Master Ching Hai

To improve the lives of all sentient beings, including that of animals...

Healthy, Cozy Doghouses

Our merciful Supreme Master Ching Hai is constantly thinking of ways to improve the lives of all sentient beings, including that of animals. Under Her careful instructions, a series of comfortable doghouses were designed to ensure warm, cozy homes for human's best friend. Each state-of-the-art doghouse boasts the following features: a non-toxic solid wood structure with offset doors for protection from wind and rain, a spacious porch covered with plexiglass sheeting material, cushioned medical-grade foam flooring for comfort, and removable windows for more air circulation in summer. The homes are also easy to assemble and to clean.

Even with such luxurious abodes for our canine friends, Master Ching Hai reminds "owners" to be sure to bring pets indoors during times of extreme heat or cold, or at night if living in dangerous zones, so the dogs will not become prey for wild animals or thieves. Actually, the dog house should be only for play and day-time, if necessary or if desired: Dogs are better inside the "owner's" house.
(For more details, please check our Website: http://www.godsdirectcontact.org.tw/eng/news/163/index2.htm, Holistic Animal Care section)

Happy Doggie-Celestial Clothes and Sleeping Mattresses for Dogs

Also per Master Ching Hai's compassionate instructions, the first-ever series of Happy Doggie Celestial Clothes and Sleeping Mattresses have been designed. These include a wide range of styles to meet the needs of dogs of all sizes. The doggie clothes are attractive in appearance and practical in their protective warmth, allowing human's loyal friends to look smart and stay warm in cold weather.

(For more details, please check our Website: http://www.godsdirectcontact.org.tw/eng/news/167/index2.htm , Holistic Animal Care section)

Food for a Healthy Doggie

Under Master Ching Hai's caring guidance, a healthy, natural and balanced vegetarian dog food was developed for our canine companions. This product is completely free of animal products and has been exclusively formulated by nutritionists. With main ingredients that include soy protein isolate, corn, oats and other grains, this wholesome and balanced diet is easy to digest and metabolize. It improves the dog's oral health and immune system and gives a glossy coat of hair, not to mention high energy levels.

Ever so thoughtful, Master Ching Hai suggests that it is better to feed freshly-prepared food to the dogs, and that ready food can be kept as an alternative when no fresh food is available or on busy days.

(For more details, please check our Website: http://www.godsdirectcontact.org.tw/eng/news/175/index.htm)

Related Information

For more information about communicating with and caring for our animal friends, along with inspiring stories from Master about Her other special animal companions, please refer to the following videotapes and DVDs.

DVD 712 The Divine Intelligence of Animals
20010605 Florida Center, U.S.A.

#714 Dogs Are Wonderful Beings
20010606 Florida Center, U.S.A.

DVD 718 Love is always good
20010607 Florida Center, U.S.A.

DVD 716 A Natural Way to Love God
20010608 Florida Center, U.S.A.

#738 Simple Living (Master & Residents)
20010426, 20010501, 20010512, 20010521 Florida Center, U.S.A.

DVD 711 The Hotel Called Life
20010623 Fresno, California, U.S.A.

#717 The Virtues Of a Good Neighbor
20010611 Florida Center, U.S.A.

#730 To Communicate by Love
20011225, 20011226 Florida Center, U.S.A.

#733 To Live with Noble Purpose
20010610 Florida Center, U.S.A.

#734 The Touch of a Master
20011226~20011227 Florida Center, U.S.A.

#740 Learning to Live in Harmony: Master's Birthday Celebration 2002
20020511 Florida Center, U.S.A.

DVD 719 Overcoming Bad Habits
20010609 Florida Center, U.S.A.

#724 Sincerity and Purity of Heart
20010612~20010616 Florida Center, U.S.A.

DVD 728 The Blessing of a Loving Thought
20011226 Florida Center, U.S.A.

#735 The Courage to Change
20011228~20011230 Florida Center, U.S.A.

DVD 755 The Laughing Saints
20030203 Florida Center, U.S.A.

DVD 756 The Value of Being Honest
20030216, 20030218 Florida Center, U.S.A.

DVD 771 A Youth's Passion
20060612

DVD 772 Laughing Through Life
20060615

DVD 773 Unconditional Devotion
20060612~20060707

DVD 780 The Dogs and the Birds in My Life

The Spiritual Teachings by The Supreme Master Ching Hai

The Key of Immediate Enlightenment
A collection of The Supreme Master Ching Hai's lectures. Available in Aulacese (1-15), Chinese (1-10), English (1-5), French (1), Finnish (1), German (1-2), Hungarian (1), Indonesian (1-5), Japanese (1-4), Korean (1-11), Mongolian (1,6), Portuguese (1-2), Polish (1-2), Spanish (1-3), Swedish (1), Thai (1-6), and Tibetan (1).

The Key of Immediate Enlightenment – Questions and Answers
A collection of questions and answers from Master's lectures.
Available in Aulacese (1-4), Bulgarian, Chinese (1-3), Czech, English (1-2), French, German, Hungarian, Indonesian (1-3), Japanese, Korean (1-4), Portuguese, Polish, and Russian.

The Key of Immediate Enlightenment – Special Edition/Seven-Day Retreat
A collection of Master's lectures in1992 during a Seven-Day Retreat in San Di Mun, Formosa. Available in English and Aulacese.

The Key of Immediate Enlightenment – Special Edition/1993 World Lecture Tour
A six-volume collection of The Supreme Master Ching Hai's lectures during the 1993 World Lecture Tour. Available in English and Chinese.

Letters Between Master and Spiritual Practitioners
Available in Aulacese (1-2), Chinese (1-3), English (1), Spanish (1)

Master Tells Stories
Available in Aulacese, Chinese, English, Japanese, Korean, Spanish, and Thai.

Of God and Humans – Insights from Bible Stories
Available in English and Chinese.

God Takes Care of Everything –
Illustrated Tales of Wisdom from The Supreme Master Ching Hai
Aulacese, Chinese, English, French, Japanese, and Korean.

The Supreme Master Ching Hai's Enlightening Humor – Your Halo Is Too Tight!
Available in Chinese and English.

Coloring Our Lives
A collection of quotes and spiritual teachings by Master. Available in Chinese and English.

Secrets to Effortless Spiritual Practice
Available in Chinese and English.

God's Direct Contact – The Way to Reach Peace
A collection of The Supreme Master Ching Hai's lectures during Her 1999 European Lecture Tour. Available in English and Chinese.

I Have Come to Take You Home
Available in Arabic, Aulacese, Bulgarian, Czech, Chinese, English, French, German, Greek, Hungarian, Indonesian, Italian, Korean, Polish, Spanish, Turkish, Romanian, and Russian.

Living in the Golden Age series
The Realization of Health – Returning to the Natural and Righteous Way of Living
Collected excerpts from the lectures of Supreme Master Ching Hai. Available in English and Chinese.

Aphorisms

Gems of eternal wisdom from Master.
Available in English/Chinese, Spanish/Portuguese, French/German, and Korean.

The Supreme Kitchen – International Vegetarian Cuisine

A collection of culinary delicacies from all parts of the world recommended by fellow practitioners.
Available in English/Chinese, Aulacese, and Japanese.

The Supreme Kitchen – Home Taste Selections

Recipes in a bilingual edition: English /Chinese.

One World... of Peace through Music

A collection of interviews and musical compositions from the 1998 benefit concert at the Shrine Auditorium in Los Angeles, California.
Trilingual edition: English/Aulacese/Chinese.

S.M. Celestial Clothes

Available in bilingual edition: English/Chinese.

The Collection of Art Creations by The Supreme Master Ching Hai – Painting Series

Through the painting of an artist, the artist's inner Self is revealed. You will be deeply touched by the intense affection, childlike innocence and motherly love of the liberated One.
Available in English and Chinese.

The Dogs in My Life (1-2)

This two-volume book set of 500 pages is a fabulous real-life set of doggy tales published by Master about Her canine companions.
Available in English and Chinese.

The Birds in My Life

In this beautifully illustrated picture-story book, Master Ching Hai shows us the secret to unlocking the animals' inner world.
Available in English and Chinese.

The Noble Wilds

The third book written *by*
Supreme Master Ching Hai

Is coming soon!

Poetry Collections by The Supreme Master Ching Hai

Wu Tzu Poems
Available in Aulacese, Chinese and English.

Silent Tears
Available in English/German/French, English/Chinese, Aulacese, Spanish, Portuguese, Korean and Filipino.

The Dream of a Butterfly
Available in Aulacese, Chinese and English.

The Old Time
Available in Aulacese and English.

Pebbles and Gold
Available in Aulacese, Chinese and English.

The Lost Memories
Available in Aulacese, Chinese and English.

Traces of Previous Lives
Available in Aulacese, English and Chinese.

Traces of Previous Lives 1, 2, 3 (CD, Video, Audio tapes) Aulacese

A Path to Love Legends 1, 2, 3 (CD, Video, Audio tapes) Aulacese

Beyond the Realm of Time (CD, DVD) Aulacese

A Touch of Fragrance (CD) Aulacese

That and This Day (CD) Aulacese

Dream in the Night (CD, DVD) Aulacese

What the Hell! (CD) Aulacese

Please Keep Forever (CD) Aulacese

Songs & Compositions of The Supreme Master Ching Hai
(CD, DVD) English, Aulacese, Chinese

Song of Love
Supreme Master Ching Hai sings timeless songs in English and Aulacese
(CD, DVD) English, Aulacese

Jeweled Verses
(CD, DVD)
Song performance and poetry recitation in Aulacese by Supreme Master Ching Hai, written by renowned Aulacese poets.

The Golden Lotus
(CD, DVD)
Aulacese poetic songs

Audio and Video Tapes

Audio tapes, DVDs, music concerts DVD, CDs, MP3s and video tapes of The Supreme Master Ching Hai's lectures and Music & Concert DVDs are available in Arabic, Armenian, Aulacese, Bulgarian, Cantonese, Cambodia, Chinese, Croatian, Czech, Danish, Dutch, English, Finnish, French, German, Greek, Hebrew, Hungarian, Indonesian, Italian, Japanese, Korean, Malay, Mongolian, Nepali, Norwegian, Mandarin, Polish, Portuguese, Persian, Russian, Romanian, Sinhalese, Slovenian, Spanish, Swedish, Thai, Turkish and Zulu. Catalog will be sent upon request. All direct inquiries are welcome.

Please visit our bookshop's website to download our catalogue and summaries of the contents of Master's latest publications:

http://www.smchbooks.com/ (in English and Chinese).

To order Master's publications,

please visit http://www.theCelestialShop.com to purchase online.

Or contact:

The Supreme Master Ching Hai International Association Publishing Co., Ltd., Taipei, Formosa

Tel: (886) 2-87873935 / Fax: (886) 2-87870873

E-mail: smchbooks@Godsdirectcontact.org

ROC Postal Remittance Account No.19259438 (for Formosa orders only)

Postal Account: : The Supreme Master Ching Hai International Association Publishing Co., Ltd.

Free Sample Booklet download

The Key of Immediate Enlightenment

(in 60 languages)

http://sb.godsdirectcontact.net/

http://www.direkter-kontakt-mit-gott.org/download/index.htm

http://www.Godsdirectcontact.org/sample/

http://www.Godsdirectcontact.us/com/sb/

How to Contact US

The Supreme Master Ching Hai International Association

P.O. Box 9, Hsihu Miaoli Hsien, Formosa (36899), R.O.C.

P.O.Box 730247, San Jose, CA 95173-0247, U.S.A.

Book Department

divine@Godsdirectcontact.org

Fax: 1-240-352-5613 / 886-949-883778

(You are welcome to join us in translating Master's books into other languages.)

The Supreme Master Ching Hai International Association Publishing Co., Ltd.

smchbooks@Godsdirectcontact.org

Tel: 886-2-87873935

Fax: 886-2-87870873

http://www.smchbooks.com

News Group

lovenews@Godsdirectcontact.org

Fax: 1-801-7409196 / 886-946-728475

Alternative Living

We Pray for You

Change Your Life
Change Your Heart
Change Your Diet

♥ ——— ♥

No more killing
Be healthy and loving

Save our Lives! We Love You

Examples of nutritious, life saving food:

Foods	Protein Concentration (Percentage by Weight)
Tofu (from soya)	16 %
Gluten (from flour)	70 %
Corn	13 %
Rice	8.6 %
Soy beans, kidney beans, chick peas, lentils, etc.	10 - 35 %
Almonds, walnuts, cashews, hazel nuts, pine nuts, etc.	14 - 30 %
Pumpkin seeds, sesame seeds, sunflower seeds, etc.	18 - 24 %

- Concentrated multi-vitamin tablets/capsules are also a good source of vitamins, minerals and anti-oxidants.
- Fruits and vegetables are full of vitamins, minerals and anti-oxidants and contain high-quality fiber for maintaining good health and a long life.
- The recommended daily allowance: 50 grams of protein (Average adult).
- Calcium from vegetables is more absorbable than from cow's milk.

- To diminish the real threat of a worldwide pandemic from bird flu,
- To avoid the danger of mad cow disease (BSE) and pig disease (PMWS), etc.
- To stop the continuing gruesome sacrifice of billions of our sweet domestic animals, marine life and feathered friends daily,

It's wise to change to a vegetarian diet for good.
It's Health
It's Economy
It's Ecology
It's Compassion
It's Peace
It's Noble

Long Life to You!

Thank You for Your Compassion

For more information, please refer to the websites listed below:
http://AL.Godsdirectcontact.org.tw/ or e-mail to AL@Godsdirectcontact.org
http://www.vegsoc.org/   http://www.vrg.org/   http://www.vegsource.com/
Supreme Master Television, airing only positive programming,
will bring a new dimension into your life.
Available worldwide as 24-hour live Internet TV at:
http://suprememastertv.com/webtv/

Inspired by the dogs
Compiled by:
The Supreme Master Ching Hai

Cameramen:
Supreme Master Ching Hai, Crystal Vo, Victor Ngo, T. June, Thomas Lux, Steven André, Danny Vu

Design and Layout:
Annie Yu, Nadir Yen, Chien Wei Ba-Li, Kim (Formosa); Jackie (Hsihu)

Graphic Design:
Gary Lai, Nadir Yen, Yu Hui-Chun, Wang Bor Tang (Formosa); Sofia, Jackie (Hsihu)

Copy Proofreading:
Lynn McGee, Jane Chu, Wenqing Li (USA); Becky Chen, Sun Wang, (Formosa);
Clair, Moon (Hsihu)

Publisher
The Supreme Master Ching Hai International Association Publishing Co., Ltd.
No 236 Soungshan Road, Taipei, Formosa, R. O. C.
Tel: 886-2-87873935
Fax: 886-2-87870873
www.smchbooks.com

The Supreme Master Ching Hai©2007
First Edition First Print: February 2007
First Edition Second Print: July 2007
First Edition Thrid Print: November 2007
Printed in Taiwan
ISBN: 978-986-6895-07-4

Spiritual Information Desk

lovewish@Godsdirectcontact.org

Fax: 886-946-730699

A Journey through Aesthetic Realms TV Program Videotapes

TV@Godsdirectcontact.org

Fax: 1-413-751-0848 (USA)

S.M. Celestial Co., Ltd.

smcj@mail.sm-cj.com

Tel: 886-2-87910860

Fax: 886-2-87911216

http://www.sm-cj.com

Celestial Shop

http://www.theCelestialShop.com

http://www.edenrules.com

Quan Yin WWW Sites

God's direct contact—The Supreme Master Ching Hai International Association's global Internet:
http://www.Godsdirectcontact.org.tw/eng/links/links.htm

This portal provides a directory of links to Quan Yin Web sites in a variety of languages, as well as 24-hour access to the TV program *A Journey through Aesthetic Realms*. You may also download multilingual editions of *The Key of Immediate Enlightenment Sample Booklet*, or download or subscribe to *The Supreme Master Ching Hai News* available in eBook or printable format, or simply browse the sites' contents online.

Supreme Master Television

Info@SupremeMasterTV.com

Tel: 1-626-444-4385

Fax: 1-626-444-4386

http://www.suprememastertv.com/

Supreme Master Television goes GLOBAL on NOV. 16, 2007
Launching on 10 NEW Satellite Platforms!
Enjoy positive, inspirational and entertaining programs
With over 30 languages and subtitles!
Free-to-Air Satellite TV channel
Also LIVE online www.SupremeMasterTV.com